Dawn and Beyond: Embark

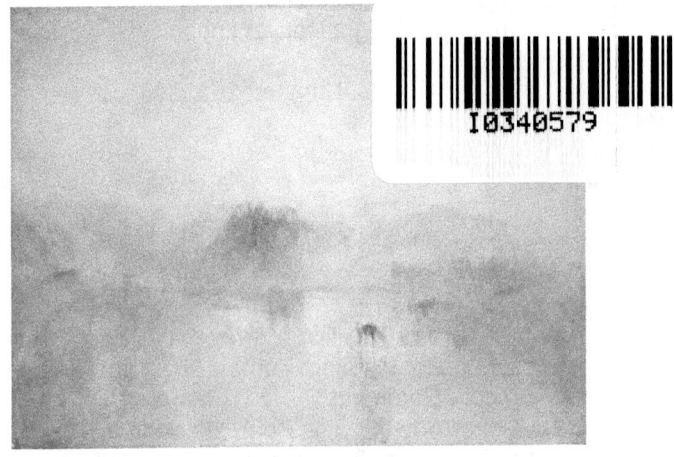

Poetry -

Come Destiny

Gary W. Burns

WWW.TURNINGCORNERBOOKS.COM

Copyright © 2023 by Turning Corner Books

Published by:
Turning Corner Books
PO Box 121
Haymarket, VA 20168

All rights reserved under International
And Pan-American Copyright Conventions.

Library of Congress Control Number: 2023903560
ISBN: 978-0-9827805-8-9

Second Printing, April 2023

Manufactured in the United States
Design by Gary W. Burns

Jacket Front Cover and Title Page Artwork: Norham Castle Sunrise, Joseph Mallord William Turner; The York Project; public domain; Wikimedia Commons.
Jacket Back Cover Artwork: The Zaan at Zaandam, Claude Monet; Private Collection, faithful photographic reproduction, public domain; Wikimedia Commons.

No part of this book may be reproduced in any form without permission in writing from the publisher; except by a reviewer, who may quote brief passages in a review to be printed in a magazine or newspaper or posted to the World Wide Web. Particular emphasis is laid on the matter of broadcasting, recording and public performance.

Dawn and Beyond: Embark

Poetry - Come Destiny

*Other Books of Poetry
by Gary W. Burns*

*Bridges: To There
(Poems for the Mind, Body & Spirit)*

*Clouds: On the Wind
(Poems for the Soul – A Meditation)*

*Earth Tones: A Journey
(Poetry for the Journey)*

*Garden Walks: Hand In Hand
(Poems To Relax By)*

*Moments: This to the Next
(Poetry - Now and Eternity)*

Poems of Love: A Selection

*Rainy Day: Wondering
(Poetry for a Rainy Day)*

To You With Love: Selected Poems

*Twilight: Awaking the Stars
(Poems of the Night's Light)*

To Kim B.

∼

*For her living
The freedom of possibility
Along the road
Destiny*

CONTENTS

Portend

Twelve	17
Begin	18
Early Morning	19
Motion	20
Numinous	21
Ponder	22
Sum	23
Fount	24
Gloriously	25
Colors	26
Taleteller	27
The Woodlot	28
Wide-Wide River	29
Collage	30
Accordingly	31
All Abloom	32
Consequently	33

Stirring

Essentially	37
Aura	38
Integral	39
Presence	40
Fields	41
Midair	42
Poets	43
Endeavor	44
Participation	45
Of Immediate	46
Progeny	47
The Flow	48
Engage	49
Fancy	50
Respite	51
Ode	52
Only To Say	53
Clothed	54
Unconditional	55

 *Awake*

Undertones	59
Winds	60
Will	61
Exploring	62
Alertness	63
Invite	64
Candlelight	65
The Choir	66
Sense	67
View	68
To Time	69
Intrinsic	70
Yet To Know	71
Ultimately	72
Serenade	73
Only Now	74
Seafaring	75
Fully	76
And Destiny	77

∞ *Integration*

Intent	81
The Tone	82
Decide	83
Integration	84
Occasion	85
Designs	86
Mockingbird	87
Kaleidoscope	88
Wisely	89
Windings	90
Plans	91
Trove	92
Primary	93
O Passer-by	94
Otherness	95
Close	96
Destined	97
Kinship	98
No Anchor	99

*Going Down the road
Of Destiny*

ଔ   ଞ

*Free-Spirited
Be*

Portend
(Dusky Dawn)

Life strikes
  the chord
    Destiny;
  We

Twelve

*On an early morning walk
I heard the wind singing
And saw many a bird winging.*

*Then
Afternoon came along
And the walk continued on
To where
A little brook ran alongside
A newly tilled field.*

*At an elbow bend
Where the brook hurried
A lone tree stood
And there
Nestling the little brook
Amply
Soft green moss grew.*

*Who would of thought
Destiny
Would bid young me,
"Rest beneath this tree
And hear me sing sweetly
"Windy Destiny"."*

Begin

Once night comes on
It takes a while
To round back
To the dusk of dawn -
Then
Sunrise,
Breaks through

Yellow-gold on blue

☙ ❧

O how wondrous
The rendezvous
That Destiny draws us to
The one where we

Come out of the blue

Early Morning

The early morning sky,
A child in its way,
Is keen
To become the full of day

ଓ ଞ

We,
Innocently free,
Sit rocking
In the lap
Of Destiny

Motion

What moves the mountains
To the sea,
What makes the sea
To be
The stormy eye
In a stormy sky

Whatever it be

It moves you
And me too

Otherwise

Destiny
Wouldn't bear true

Numinous

The day,
In its dusky-dawn way,
Has coaxed
The landscape to appear

And what was away
In the dark
Is once again
Near

ɑ̃   ʚ

Bud
And bloom

Have ever been
Destiny within

Ponder

The premise of Life
The spectrum of Things

☙ ❧

The Destiny
We weigh
Day to day

Sum

A mist passed through the morning
Just enough to dampen things

Spring

The young mockingbird sings
Long into the night

        ଔ   ଙ

Looking Destiny
    eye to eye,
We come to live
    we go to die

Fount

Vast
The wellspring of feelings
The multitude of thoughts

        ॐ   ॐ

In the house
Of Now

Where emotion stirs
And thoughts
Linger

The songs
Of Destiny
Are sung
By the spirited singer

Gloriously

Wild roses,
Gloriously abundant

        ଔ   ଞ

We

Inward living
Humanity

Outward surmounting
Destiny

Colors

*The rainbow
That was there
But a moment ago*

Gone

                ඥ   ఠ

*All's about, till
Off all goes
Into the thin air
Of the somewhere,*

Of Destiny

*Think to live
Attentively*

Taleteller

*She flew
And he flew too
From dogwood
To elder*

*Bathed in sunshine
The marigolds
Go
From bud to bloom
And run
Through yellow to gold*

༺ ༻

*Gathered by eyes
That see scenery old
Young images
Unfold*

*The tale of Destiny
Told*

The Woodlot

In the woodlot,
Springtide -

All in a hurry
A flurry

Dove, junco, sparrow,
Cardinal, wren
And woodlot squirrel too

        ର   ଓ

Dressed
In the how
     of now

The inevitability
     of destiny
Woos
     Infinity

Wide - Wide River

Blue is blue
        & rain is rain

But
As the day goes by
Blue differs in the sky

And no drop of rain
Is the same

        ଔ   ଛ

Destiny,
The fountainhead
Of imagination

Fosters
The wide-wide river
Creation

Collage

The years
Gracefully escorting me
I pursue
Warmheartedly

ଔ ଓ

Lighting life,
By way
Of ever changing scenery,
Destiny's collage
Watchfully

Discerns you and me

Accordingly

*Does the tick-tock of a clock
Make time*

*Do heart and mind
Afford rhythm and rhyme*

ଓ ଓ

*Destiny
Unable to inform me
Of the intentions of infinity*

*Challenges me
With
"Ask thyself,
Which way
Will your path be"*

*And from there
I move accordingly*

All Abloom

*This morning
In the magnolia tree
All abloom,
The gray catbird sang
Many a tune*

*Now
As ebony
Soaks into the gray*

Night's on its way

            ɔ̃   ʚ

*What flower
Grows by sight
And blooms by touch*

*The one that opens at night
The one needed so much;*

*O Destiny's bloom
Filling the world
In but a room*

Consequently

A gusty wind -

Leaf shadows flutter
Beneath the maple tree
As wild flowers sway
Off in the lea

        ଔ   ଓ

As the whirling wind
Spun about me
I overheard it say
To the in flight blue jay

"In coming
You're going

Consequently

Be
Is your destiny"

Stirring
(Sunrise)

*Leave it to the rowdy blue jay
To wake up the day*

Essentially

Essentially

I can tell of me
Only

You of you

            ର   ଛ

What you give

In the name of Live

Will be
Your destiny

Aura

Clear blue sky
Sunray

Clouds of gray
Rain today

                ఇ   ఞ

Omni
Destiny

Eternity

Integral

The morning sun
Moves across
The nighttime frost

And while trumpeting
The morning view

Turns the clinging frost
To watery dew

ଔ ଓ

Be one
With you

And to you
Destiny will ring true

Presence

The piper on the sand
At the edge of the sea,
Prints
Left
Momentarily,

Wave by wave
Washed away

O the Sea of Eternity

ଔ ଓ

Swish we;
The Water of Life,
Destiny

Fields

The river Time
Leaves
Thoughtful tracks behind;

From spacious banks
Fishing folk fish

And in swift currents
Swimmers swim

ଔ   ଖ

Waterfalls
Aim spring thaws
Towards waiting fields

There
Rivulets
At the fields behest

Set the flow free
To possibility

Midair

A humming bird landed
On the honeysuckle vine

Rested
It took to midair
And glanced at me
While hovering there

Then
It quickly left
To declare
Its presence
Elsewhere

ଓଃ ଙ

Taking you
And taking me
Destiny wings us
Eternally

Poets

A crescendo of blue
Plays through
The morning sky

As crystal-clear dew
Readies anew
To rise high

        ଘ   ଓ

Destiny

Sets free
The poetry
Of Be

Endeavor

We influence fate
With each endeavor

Then, now
And ever

        ಌ   ಏ

Amidst future
And past

In now
We last

Participation

In a dance
Called Mystery
A mysterious mist
Moves over the swaying sea

ଔ ଶ

Knowing not
The mysteries of
Birth nor death

Willingly
Life courts breath

Of Immediate

The hours till our meeting
Unfold

Now
Me your hands hold

        ଔ   ഇ

Future heralds you
Future heralds me

Immediate

Is our destiny

Progeny

A turn comes
The turn's made

Turn,
The Father of everything

        ও   ৡ

Being the matrix
Of Infinity

She's rather elusive
Old Destiny

The Flow

*There's controversy
Upon the breeze
There's chatter
Among the leaves*

*By sunshine
There're told
A whoosh when young
A rattle when old*

 ❧   ☙

*We,
The rain falling,
Into the river
Go*

*Destiny
The flow*

Engage

The day's heat
The night's chill
The rhythm of seasons

The voice of time - "we"
The rhyme

        ଔ   ஐ

Destiny:
Intention
      sailing the sea
           of Discovery

Fancy

*With nothing
In pursuit
Rivers run
To where the source
Knows not*

        ღ   ღ

*We
In our fancy run*

Come destiny

Respite

O how the flame
Toils;

Leaving
Some light for tomorrow
To help me find my way

I'll put out the candle
For today

ଔ   ঌ

On the pages of reality
Destiny
Vividly
Tells the story
Of you and me

Ode

The clear sky
Of a summer's day
Gives way
To the clouds that roam

Days
Knowing you
Nor I
Go by

ଔ ଓ

If Now
Is Eternity

What must Destiny be

Only To Say

The pond
Where once the dairy herd
Would come to drink
Is now clod filled
And a field

And the once eager brook
Is but a trickle

ଔ ଓ

Celebrate the day
In the day

For Destiny
Comes only to say,
I'm here today
Then gone away

Clothed

*Clouds
Clothe the night
As they do the day,*

*Patiently
Watch the scenery*

☙ ❧

*Dressed in Destiny
Willingly*

*We navigate
Our history*

Unconditional

Never burning
Twice the same
The flame

        ଓ   ଽ

Me absorbing the day,
The day absorbing me -
Staying
Going

Unconditionally

Awake
(Sunshine)

*Courage to be
 your Destiny
Along paths
 of possibility*

Undertones

Dawn's gone,
Day's dressed in dim

Streaks of cloudy gray
Run through sky-blue

      ଓ   ଥ

Destiny calls to us
Hinting

And we answer
Being

Winds

Whirling,

In the windy mind
There's a choice you'll find

      ଓ   ଚ

Winds shape

Contour of land,
Crest of sea,
Cloud of sky

Destiny
And be

Will

On a crisp day in autumn

Leaves
Brown
Upon the ground

Await the winter snow

        ☙ ❧

Willingly -

I go decidedly
To where my going
        takes me

I know of no other way
        to be free

Exploring

Through the hot summer
The sun sweeps
The sky wide
In search of twilight dusk

Through the snowy winter
The sun
In a smaller sweep
Seeks as much

ଔ ୭

Living inhales
The air of strife
Destiny exhales
The breath of life

Alertness

Water
Shimmering
Sun

        ଔ   ଓ

Being
Destiny

The now of here
Holds me

Eternally

Invite

*I'm not sure
Of the origination
Of the invitation
But, July is here*

ଓଃ ଞ

*In the archway
Of liminality*

*We
Mirror Destiny*

Candlelight

*From remnants
Of aromatic wax
We make
New candles*

      ଔ   ଏ

*Wick
Soul
Flame
Spirit
Fragrance
Life*

The Choir

Today on a walk
Through a picturesque park
Where I stayed
Till long after dark

Welcoming scenes
Came and went

Sprawling showy
Gardens

Spewing sporadic
Fountains

People
Everywhere

ଔ ଓ

Destiny
Sings its song
To which we chorus along

Sense

*Autumn's leaves
Are holding on this year,
A rainy spring
Ably helped them here*

*Today,
Clouds layered on clouds
Honeycomb the sky
And the tall trees
In a brisk breeze
Are rocking*

ଓ ଛ

*The flow that is to be,
The one named Destiny,*

*Forms the formless
Imaginatively*

View

Shepherding time
The tending mind
Lives life

And O
The scenery
That be

Forest, sky, sea
City walk, scraper high
Country lane, river bend
Land's end

ଓଃ ଽଠ

Destiny
In darkness be;
Now
Proffers reality

To Time

A thief
Stole time that was mine

When caught
I'd come to find

I gave the thief
My time

And
There was no crime

ଓ ଶ

Of Destiny's
Yearning burning -

Are the embers dying
Or are they
The hidden glow
Of tomorrow

Intrinsic

*On a sultry
Summer day*

*Clouds
Voicing loud,
Via thunder storm,
Set the sky aglow*

*With streaks
Of yellow*

       ଓ   ଏ

*Lived,
Destiny
Has a tendency
To follow me*

Yet To Know

Down
From a cloudless sky
A crystal blue
Streams though
The picture window

Outside,
A colorful medley
All a flush
For an artist's brush

        ଔ   ೞ

Who knows what disguise
Is worn by the eyes
As cloudless skies lay open
What's out there
In Destiny's lair

Ultimately

Life sings
What your will
Brings

        ଔ   ୬

As we live
Destiny
Gives all
It has to give

Serenade

The skies, our eyes
A gaze

The sun, the stars
A blaze

You, me
The earth, the sea

Singing
Eternity

ಌ ಐ

Love
Is the gate
Through which
The joys of Destiny
Celebrate

The life We create

Only Now

Four cups of coffee

*It's a frosty
Mid-October
Morning*

ଓ ଔ

*Not waiting for me
Destiny*

Running ahead

*Made plans
That Only Now
I know to be
My destiny*

Seafaring

Rhythmic heart

Ebb and flow
We go

ଔ ଓ

Life
Buoy's
Upon the current
Destiny

Fully

I gathered my self

Came home to me

And there found,
 waiting,
Destiny

        ଓ   ଚ

Tomorrow's destiny
Is lived
Today
In every way

And Destiny

Trekking the mountain side,

Snows fall -

Listening

Winds whisper

      ଓ   ଔ

By birth we are betrothed
By breath wedded

We
And Destiny

Integration
(Stardust)

*In a starlit sky
A learned owl
Flew by*

Intent

*This morning the winds
Blew
And the morning dew
Went away*

*This noon
The hard winds
Set the trees to sway*

*This evening
Here we are, me
Along with you
Awaiting the sunset view*

ଔ ଷ

*As the images of the day
Fade away
And the swell of imagery
Dwell
In the world of intra-*

*The winds of Intent
Blow with Destiny's
Consent*

The Tone

The snow
*   falling*
*   falling*

Fallen deep

O how hauntingly beautiful

The smoothness
Of the blanketed landscape

Still

          ღ   ღ

Destined

If it's in you
It's found

Decide

The last leaves
Were blown quickly
From the now naked trees,

Air perfumed
With leafy scented mist,

Outside a late-late fall storm

Early scenes of winter born

༄ ༅

Destiny:
Decisions that
Determine the
Design of our lives

Integration

Sunshine,
Golden umbrella

Cloudscape,
Dreams of tomorrow

Raindrops,
Life growing

Moonglow,
Midnight meadow

ଔ ଓ

Sensing an affinity
With Destiny
Whole longs to be

Occasion

*Daylight melts
Into the dark of night*

*Shadows
In soft moonlight
Hold dreamy hours tight*

*Union wins
The dream begins*

ଔ ஐ

*Eagerly
Destiny
Begets Eternity*

Designs

Down a busy boulevard
Across a teeming crosswalk
Then, on
Into the wine bar

There,
Laughter
Dancing
On a glass of wine

ଔ   ଓ

Through solitary days
And days
Filled with people too

We design ways
To pursue
Destiny in Do

Mockingbird

While feeding the mockingbird
Through the harsh winter
I thought

Come summer
Will you sing for me,

Fleeting
Place to place
Where's home
For the mockingbird
Or you or me

ଔ ଛ

Is my only true home
Your eyes
As you see me now,

Who knows
What life will bring

And if
The mockingbird will sing

Kaleidoscope

The kaleidoscope
Of mind
Entwines

        ଓ   ଶ

Destiny,
By our design,
Moves steadily
Through the hands
Of the Sands
             of Time

Wisely

Things go away
Imparting memories
For today

        ଔ   ଊ

The echo of Destiny,
Memory

Windings

I noticed a reflection tonight
I'd never noticed before

There was a glow
On the knob of the door

༒ ༒

Destiny

Confronting you and me
At the edge of mortality,
Calls out

"The journey
Lives in Be!"

Plans

Clouds move over the sun
Variations of brightness ensue

      ଔ   ଓ

What's seeable
We see

What's not
We imagine to be,

Destiny's creativity

Trove

Earthbound
The melting snow
Reveals the evergreen's
Green

    ଔ ஐ

The heart beats
And Destiny
Keeps going away

O the treasure
Of living
In today

Primary

Red takes the heart
From flame to love

Blue takes the mind
From sky to sea

Yellow sun
Unfolds scenery

ଔ ୫ଠ

Come destiny

In the womb
Of the wind
We begin

O Passers-by

Blue, sliver, pink
Reddish orange, yellow
Tints of gold
Golden, gone

Sunset sky
Goodbye

ଔ ଓ

In quest,

Mountain spring

To valley river

To Sea of Destiny

Otherness

Deep woods,
Dressed dim
In moonlit shadows,
Speak
In murmuring tones

ങ ഊ

What don't we see

Courting

Destiny

Close

It's mid-February,
Three robins
Perch atop an old oak

There
They await the brooding Spring
Where they'll sing
For the sake of the hatchling

ଘ ଓ

We gather voices from
Outside
But
They have to be
Inside
For us to hear,

O how close
We are

In the destinies
We hold dear

Destined

The sun's setting
Over there
Without a care

ଓଃ ଽଠ

Li Po drank his wine
And I drink mine

Did I find him
Or did he
Find me

Whichever

Now we be
The destined of destiny

Kinship

Winter rains came
And washed away
The robins nest

To the robins
No matter
The young
Have long gone

ଔ ୬୦

Destiny,
Dressed in foresee,
Claims kin to reality

No Anchor

Stars all alight
Illumine
The universe of night

        ଔ   ଓ

As you sail with me
Bids the anchorless ship
Destiny

Hold firm the helm

For the winds
Don't ask your name

To them
It's all the same

Take courage

           Sail on

About the Author

Inspired by nature and the beauty around him the multi-award winning poet Gary W. Burns started writing poetry at a young age. Early on Gary was able to express his thoughts, ideas and emotions through the vivid imagery of his verse. His poetry has been published in various literary arts journals, anthologies and magazines. He is the author of 10 books of poetry. Through his poems Gary shares his reflections on the many facets of life and on the beauty of nature. The expressiveness of his poetry has been enriched by his wide reading in philosophy and psychology. He has traveled throughout the world and has lived in numerous countries, to include, Italy, Korea, Saudi Arabia and Canada. He has also lived in Hawaii and several other states. Currently, Gary makes his home in Northern Virginia near the foothills of the Blue Ridge Mountains

ENJOY THESE OTHER BOOKS OF POETRY BY GARY W. BURNS

Clouds: On the Wind
(Poems for the Soul - A Meditation)
ISBN: 978-0-9845342-0-2 (Paperback)
ISBN: 978-0-9845342-1-0 (Hardcover)
ISBN: 978-0-9860900-3-5 (E-Book)

Bridges: To There
(Poems for the Mind, Body & Spirit)
ISBN: 978-0-9827805-6-5 (Paperback)
ISBN: 978-0-9827805-7-2 (Hardcover)
ISBN: 978-0-9860900-3-5 (E-Book)

Garden Walks: Hand In Hand
(Poems To Relax By)
ISBN: 978-0-9845342-3-4 (Paperback)
ISBN: 978-0-9827805-0-3 (Hardcover)
ISBN: 978-0-9860900-1-1 (E-Book)

Available wherever books are sold.

Earth Tones: A Journey
(Poetry for the Journey)
ISBN: 978-0-9845342-6-5 (Paperback)
ISBN: 978-0-9845342-9-6 (Hardcover)
ISBN: 978-0-9860900-8-0 (E-Book)

Moments: This to the Next
(Poetry - Now and Eternity)
ISBN: 978-0-9845342-4-1 (Paperback)
ISBN: 978-0-9827805-1-0 (Hardcover)
ISBN: 978-0-9860900-9-7 (E-Book)

Rainy Day: Wondering
(Poems for a Rainy Day)
ISBN: 978-0-9845342-5-8 (Paperback)
ISBN: 978-0-9827805-2-7 (Hardcover)
ISBN: 978-0-9860900-7-3 (E-Book)

Available wherever books are sold.

To You With Love: Selected Poems
ISBN: 978-0-9845342-6-5 (Paperback)
ISBN: 978-0-9827805-3-4 (Hardcover)
ISBN: 978-0-9860900-2-8 (E-Book)

Twilight: Awaking the Stars
(Poems of the Night's Light)
ISBN: 978-0-9845342-7-2 (Paperback)
ISBN: 978-0-9827805-4-1 (Hardcover)
ISBN: 978-0-9860900-6-6 (E-Book))

Poems of Love: A Selection
ISBN: 978-0-9845342-8-9 (Paperback)
ISBN: 978-0-9827805-5-8 (Hardcover)
ISBN: 978-0-9860900-5-9 (E-Book)

Available wherever books are sold.

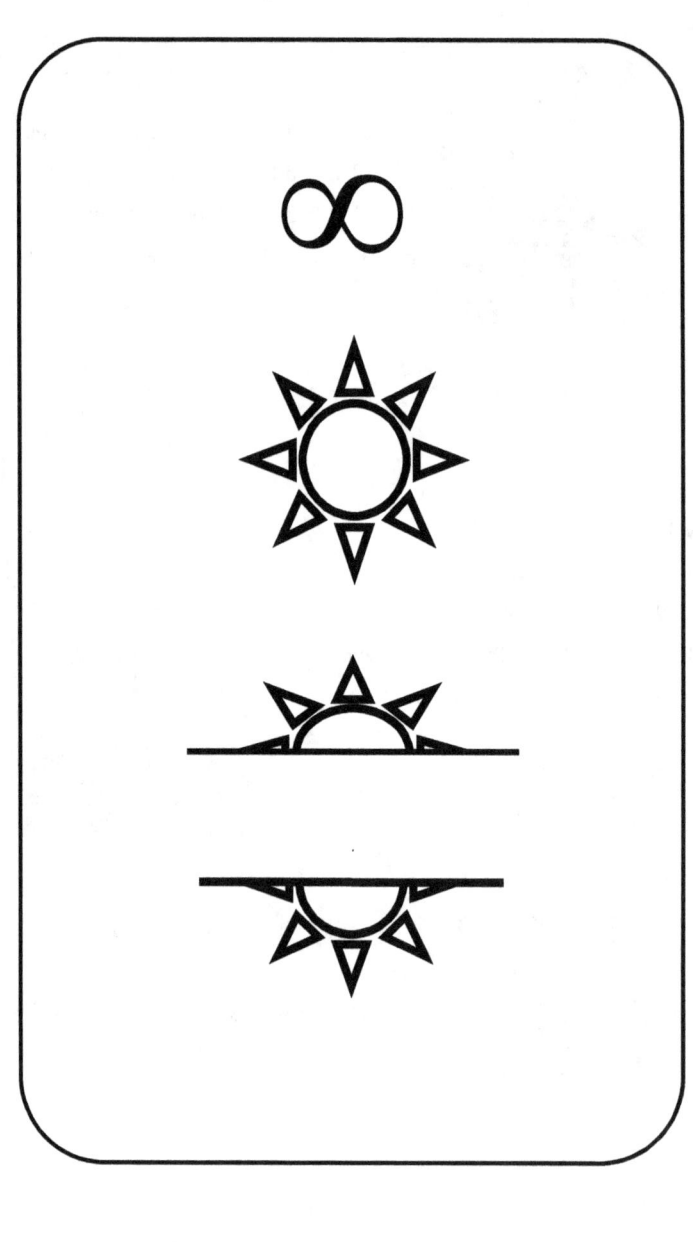

www.ingramcontent.com/pod-product-compliance
Lightning Source LLC
Chambersburg PA
CBHW072059290426
44110CB00014B/1743